モギケンの英語シャワーBOX 実践版
茂木健一郎

STEP

2

朝日出版社

Contents

CDブックの構成と使い方 _____ 4

7. バックグラウンド・トゥ・ブリテン _____ 8
   Background to Britain

8. 国のない男 _____ 20
   A Man Without a Country

9. オバマ演説集 _____ 32
   The Speeches of Barack Obama

10. 選択の自由 _____ 46
    Free to Choose

11. 三四郎 _____ 56
    Sanshirō

12. 賢者の贈りもの _____ 64
    The Gift of the Magi

13. 魔女のパン _____ 72
    Witches' Loaves

14. 最後の一葉 _____ 80
    The Last Leaf

Column
「ネイティブ」信仰の呪縛から逃れ、"自由に"英語で表現する _____ 54

CDブックの構成と使い方

3STEPで段階的にレベルアップ

このCDブックは、次の3つのステップで段階的にレベルアップできるように構成してあります。

STEP1 HOP

ピーターラビット・シリーズや『星の王子さま』など、絵本や子供向けの作品から、大人でも十分に楽しめる『赤毛のアン』といった作品が収録されています。子供向けであっても一口に簡単とは言えませんが、ネイティブが子供の頃に読んできた作品に触れることで、まずは英語シャワーに慣れてください。

STEP2 STEP

大人向けの英語から、比較的読みやすいものをセレクトしました。僕が学生時代にテキストとして使った『Background to Britain』やオバマ大統領の演説、オー・ヘンリーの短編などが収録されています。中学英語を勉強した人であれば、それほど難しくない作品ばかりだと思います。英語シャワーの「流れ」を感じられるように読んでみてください。

STEP3 JUMP

『老人と海』や『風と共に去りぬ』など、ネイティブの大人が読む小説なので、少々手強いかもしれませんが、どれも僕が読んで感動した名作ばかりです。和訳で読んだことのある作品からチャレンジすれば、多少わからないところがあっても、英語の"美味しさ"を味わえるのではないかと思います。

作品の難易度

それぞれの作品の最初のページに、難易度を星のマークで示してあります。星の数が多いほど、英語のレベルが高くなりますが、必ずしも **STEP1** が星一つとは限りません。読むときの目安にしてください。

- 難易度 ★☆☆　比較的簡単
- 難易度 ★★☆　それほど難しくない
- 難易度 ★★★　チャレンジしがいがあり

CDブックの構成と使い方

CDブックの使い方

作品の「内容」または「あらすじ」を読んだ後、鑑賞のヒントとなる日本語のエッセイを読みながら、対応する部分の Scene の原文にチャレンジしてください。

まず最初は、赤い下敷きを重ねて、わからない単語があっても流れを止めずに、最後まで読んでください。次に、本を見ながら朗読CDを聞いた後、今度は自分で声に出して何度か読んでみます。そして最後に下敷きを取り、知りたい単語をチェックします。

❶ 内容またはあらすじをチェックする
❷ エッセイを読みながら、原文にチャレンジする
❸ 朗読CDを聞く
❹ 声に出して読む
❺ わからない単語を確認する

7. Background to Britain

8. A Man Without a Country

9. The Speeches of Barack Obama

10. Free to Choose

11. Sanshirō

12. The Gift of the Magi

13. Witches' Loaves

14. The Last Leaf

7 Background to Britain

イギリス文化への興味を芽生えさせてくれた最初の英文テキスト

> 原題 Background to Britain
> 著者 M. D. Munro Mackenzie, L. J. Westwood
> 発表 1965年
> 内容：イギリスの文化を愛情とユーモアを交えながら紹介したテキスト。食、スポーツ、テレビ、パブなど現代のイギリス人の日常生活にまつわるさまざまなテーマについて、簡潔な英語で紹介されている。

語学を学ぶ上で大切な、最初のテキスト

　僕が高校一年生だった頃のことです。これから夏季休暇に入る生徒たちに、当時の高校の先生が一冊の薄い本を配布しました。タイトルは "Background to Britain"。二人のイギリス人によって書かれたこの本は、僕のイギリスに対する興味に最初の灯りを点じました。

　ある語学を学ぼうとするとき、どのようなテキストを用いるかというのは、とても大切な問題です。優れた文章を読めば、自然とその背後の文化にまで惹きつけられますが、そうでなければ語学

のみならず、その国そのものに対する興味も失ってしまうからです。その意味で、この "Background to Britain" は、英語を学び始めたばかりの僕にとって、この上なく素晴らしいテキストでした。

　書き手である二人のイギリス人は、優れた英語の文章を僕らに教えてくれただけではなく、彼らの母国イギリスの文化を、深い愛情とユーモアを交えながら紹介してくれたのです。

書き込みでボロボロになった本

　冊子を開くと、イギリス人の日常生活にまつわるさまざまなテーマが紹介されています。"Going to the theatre"、"Pubs"、"Public holidays"、"Sport"、"T.V."、"English food" などなど。

　たとえば、"Lunch in Town" のテーマでは、ロンドンの都会で働く人々がどのようにランチタイムを過ごしているのかが語られています。夏になると公園で催されるランチタイムのコンサートを聴きながら、サンドイッチをほおばる人の姿が見られることなど、まだ一度も海外に行ったことのない僕たちにとっては、大いに想像力をかき立てられたものでした。

　英語を学ぶときは「辞書を引かない」主義の僕も、その頃はまだ英語の勉強法が確立されていませんでした。ボロボロになったこの冊子を開くと、ところどころに日本語の意味が書き込まれて

います。「この頃はこんな簡単な単語がわからなかったのかぁ」と、当時が懐かしく思い返されます。

異国の"空気"を肌で感じる

　一つ一つのテーマは短く、文章も極めて簡潔。知らない単語も前後の文脈でほとんどすべて推察できるので、ボキャブラリーにとらわれずにイギリスの庶民の暮らしの"空気"を肌で感じ取ってみてください。

　ここでは、三つのテーマをご紹介します。一つ目は "The Cockney"。"The Cockney accent" とはいわゆる「ロンドン英語」のことで、その特徴としては、例えばtoday「トゥデイ」を「トゥダイ」と発音したりします。 Scene1 ではロンドンの下町っ子のユーモアを重んじる気質、言葉の特徴などが綴られています。

　 Scene2 の "London's parks" ではロンドンの街の至るところにある、緑豊かな公園と、それぞれの魅力や楽しみ方などが紹介されています。

　そして Scene3 は、イギリスが誇る大詩人、大戯曲家であるウィリアム・シェイクスピアについて語られた "Shakespeare" です。

Background to Britain

Scene 1 The Cockney

Almost everyone who has heard of London has heard of the term "Cockney". Strictly speaking, in order to call oneself a Cockney one should have been born "within the sound of Bow bells", that is to say within the sound of the bells of the church of St Mary-le-Bow, which stands nearly in the centre of the City of London. But, in fact, all London's citizens who were born and bred in the city may call themselves Cockneys if they wish. However, the term is generally reserved for the Londoner with a "Cockney accent".

The Cockney accent is not a particularly pleasant or melodious one, and the Cockney's distortion of the English language is such that the foreigner often finds it impossible to understand the speaker until his ear has become acclimatised to the peculiar tones. The principal characteristics of the Cockney accent consist in a general slurring of consonants (the aspirate aitch is often ignored) and a distortion of vowel sounds. The best known example of Cockney speech in modern English literature is that of Eliza Doolittle, the heroine of Bernard Shaw's play, *Pygmalion* and of the musical adapted from it, *My Fair Lady*.

But if Cockney speech is unpleasant, the Cockney himself is usually far from being so. The average Cockney is distinguished by his quick wit, his ready sense of humour, his ability to "carry on" under unusual or difficult conditions and by his willingness to be of help if he can. The Cockney's humour is often satirical but it is never vicious; he is very ready to laugh at other people's peculiarities but he is equally ready to laugh at his own. He often makes jokes under the most difficult conditions, a quality that was very apparent during World War II. This rather lugubrious type of humour is well exemplified by the title of an old Cockney music-hall song: "Ain't It Grand To Be Blooming Well Dead".

Nowadays, as the tempo of life in big cities grows ever faster (although the Cockney opposes this process when he can), the opportunities for the Cockney to exercise his wit and humour diminish. But if one keeps one's ears open on buses, in railway stations, in street markets and similar places, it will soon become evident that the spirit of Cockney humour is still very much alive, although the old Cockney pronunciation is less common than hitherto.

Most people who call themselves Cockneys usually do so with some pride. And, by and large, they are justified.

Scene2 London's parks

One thing about London which every visitor from abroad admires is the large number of parks. These "lungs" of London, as they have been called, are like green islands of peace and quiet in the middle of a noisy sea. They play an important part in helping to form the city's character.

The best-known parks are, of course, the central ones: St James's Park, Hyde Park, Regent's Park, and Kensington Gardens. They have many attractions. Hyde Park has the Serpentine, a little lake, where, if one feels inclined, one may take a swim or go for a row, and Speakers' Corner where one may get up and say anything (or almost anything!) one pleases. In Regent's Park there are the Zoo and the Open-Air Theatre. Kensington Gardens has the Round Pond where "dry land sailors" of all ages sail every kind of model yacht. St James's Park boasts a truly elegant lake on which lives a great variety of wild duck. And, apart from these individual attractions, each park has a greater or lesser expanse of well-kept grass. Here, in fine weather, can be seen hundreds of lucky people who have escaped for a while from the noise and bustle of the town; some sitting on chairs, some lying full length on the ground, some strolling aimlessly around.

But the central parks of London are not necessarily the most popular. Every district of London has its parks, great or small. In the north there is Hampstead Heath, famous for its summer and winter fairs. In the south there is Richmond Park, where deer and sheep still roam and where one can get the impression of being deep in the country. In the south, too, are the Botanical Gardens at Kew, where almost every kind of tree and plant is carefully tended, in large greenhouses or in the open air. Just over Chelsea Bridge, along the south bank of the Thames, is Battersea Park, one of London's largest, complete with its Pleasure Gardens and Fun-Fair. In the east, there is the large Victoria Park and a host of smaller ones.

And so one could go on. Even for a Londoner it is difficult to know and enjoy them all. The visitor to the city may be confident that wherever he is, he is not far away from a park of some description which waits to offer him the same pleasures and relaxations that it does to the Londoner.

Scene3 Shakespeare

For any Englishman, there can never be any discussion as to who is the world's greatest poet and greatest dramatist. Only one name can possibly suggest itself to him: that of William Shakespeare. Every Englishman has some knowledge, however slight, of the work of our greatest writer. All of us use words, phrases and quotations from Shakespeare's writings that have become part of the common property of English-speaking people. Most of the time we are probably unaware of the source of the words we use, rather like the old lady who was taken to see a performance of *Hamlet* and complained that "it was full of well-known proverbs and quotations"!

Shakespeare, more perhaps than any other writer, made full use of the great resources of the English language. Most of us use about five thousand words in our normal employment of English; Shakespeare in his works used about twenty-five thousand! There is probably no better way for a foreigner (or an Englishman!) to appreciate the richness and variety of the English language than by studying the various ways in which Shakespeare uses it. Such a study is well worth the effort (it is not, of course, recommended to beginners), even though some aspects of English usage, and the meaning of many words, have changed since Shakespeare's day.

It is paradoxical that we should know comparatively little about the life of the greatest English author. We know that Shakespeare was born in 1564 in Stratford-on-Avon, and that he died there in 1616. He almost certainly attended the Grammar School in the town, but of this we cannot be sure. We know he was married there in 1582 to Anne Hathaway and that he had three children, a boy and two girls. We know that he spent much of his life in London writing his masterpieces. But this is almost all that we do know.

However, what is important about Shakespeare's life is not its incidental details but its products, the plays and the poems. For many years scholars have been trying to add a few facts about Shakespeare's life to the small number we already possess and for an equally long time critics have been theorising about the plays. Sometimes, indeed, it seems that the poetry of Shakespeare will disappear beneath the great mass of comment that has been written upon it.

Fortunately this is not likely to happen. Shakespeare's poetry and Shakespeare's people (Macbeth, Othello, Hamlet, Falstaff and all the others) have long delighted not just the English but lovers of literature everywhere, and will continue to do so after the scholars and commentators and all their works have been forgotten.

8 国のない男

難易度 ★☆☆

「科学的思考」を文学の中に取り入れた、アメリカを代表する作家の遺作

> 原題 A Man Without a Country
> 著者 Kurt Vonnegut
> 発表 2005年
> 内容：カート・ヴォネガットの遺作で、往年の読者を広く越え話題となったエッセイ集。徹底的なアメリカ批判、現代文明批判、独自の文学観、芸術観、人間観、音楽への愛を独特のユーモアとシニカルさをもって語っている。

『ライ麦畑でつかまえて』を超える人気

　作者のカート・ヴォネガット（Kurt Vonnegut）は、何を書いてもベストセラーが保証される、二十世紀後半のアメリカ現代文学を代表する大作家の一人です。

　コーネル大学では化学を専攻し、その作品にはＳＦ的なアイデアが多用されていることから、ある時期まではＳＦ作家と称されていましたが、本人はそう呼ばれることを苦々しく思っていたようです。一方で、現代の作家が科学技術について無知であること

を「テクノロジーをろくに書き込んでいない小説は、現代の人間を描き切れていない」と批判しています。

ヴォネガットは科学的思考を文学の中に取り入れたことでＳＦ作家というレッテルづけをされ、文壇からは無視され、長く不遇の時代を経験しました。しかしその後、アメリカの大学生のあいだで熱狂的に読まれ、1969年に第二次世界大戦での自身の捕虜体験を描いた『スローターハウス5』を発表したことで一躍注目を浴び、現代アメリカ作家としての決定的な評価を得ることとなったのです。

今でも『スローターハウス5』は、サリンジャーの『ライ麦畑でつかまえて』を超えてアメリカのティーンエージャーに支持されています。

『国のない男』がアメリカで出版された二年後、2007年1月のインタビューでヴォネガットは「これが最後の一冊になる」ことを明言しています。そして、その年の春に八十四歳で亡くなったため、その言葉通り彼の遺作となりました。

英会話上達のための、意外な近道

ヴォネガットの作品は宇宙的視野を取り入れ、その中にナンセンスなギャグや寓話を散りばめたユニークな発想と、作品に込め

られた強烈な風刺や逆説そして、その陰に隠された温かなユーモアが特徴的です。

Scene1 は子どもが言語を学んでいく過程について書かれています。子どもが言語を習得していくためには、周りの会話に耳を澄ませ、わからない言葉には勘を働かせて意味を推測し、タイミングを計り、会話に加わるしかありません。その会話に加わるために大事なのがジョークなのだと言っています。

それは僕が身をもって経験したことでもあります。高校一年生の夏休みに、英会話もろくにできない状態で初めて海外へ行き、あるホームパーティーに参加しました。僕だけが日本人で、あとはネイティブの人ばかりという場でしたが、日本人だからといって誰も手加減はしてくれませんでした。そこで僕がどうやって会話に加わったかというと、複雑なことは言えないので、短いジョークを言って周りを笑わせたのです。

この経験で僕の会話力はものすごく鍛えられました。ですから、まだ英語があまり得意ではないという人もまずは短いジョークが言えるようになると、急激に上達するのではないかと思います。

笑いは、逆境を乗り越えるための力

ヴォネガットは「ユーモアとは、恐怖に対する生理的な反応」

だと言っています。つまり、笑いとは「逆境を乗り越えるために人類が獲得してきた、物事をポジティブに変換できる力」だと。彼は、ドレスデン大空襲で焼け野原になった街を見て笑いますが、それは捨て鉢になって笑ったのではありません。絶望的な状況においても、人間の心の底に潜んでいる「生きる力」を促してくれるのが、このユーモアだと言っているのです。

「国のない男」になった理由

　一方で本書では、徹底的なアメリカ批判を行っています。そしてアメリカにおいてもっとも許しがたい反逆は、「アメリカ人は愛されていない」という言葉を口にすることだと皮肉っています。アメリカという国の面白さは、自由や正義というある種の傲慢さを振りかざす一方で、ヴォネガットやチョムスキーのような良心的な知識人が存在していることです。 Scene2

　「われわれはいま世界中の人々から、かつてのナチスと同じくらい恐れられ、憎まれている」というように、本書はアメリカや現代文明に対するシニカルさで溢れています。環境破壊を憂い、アメリカの現状を憂い、そして自ら母国を見限る。ゆえにヴォネガットは「国のない男」となったのです。そして彼はそれらに対してユーモアとシニカルさで立ち向かっています。ユーモアがある

からこそ、単なる"アンチ"にとどまらないのでしょう。

　ヴォネガットは、自身が繰り返して表明しているとおり、徹底した悲観論者です。にもかかわらず、彼の語り口には自嘲的な冷徹さが感じられません。それは、最大の笑いは、最大の絶望や不安に根ざしていると考え、どんな悲惨な状況でも決してユーモアを忘れない気持ちが温かな語り口となって現れているからなのでしょう。 Scene3

A Man Without a Country

国のない男

Scene 1　CD2-4

As a kid I was the youngest member of my family, and the youngest child in any family is always a jokemaker, because a joke is the only way he can enter into an adult conversation. My sister was five years older than I was, my brother was nine years older than I was, and my parents were both talkers. So at the dinner table when I was very young, I was boring to all those other people. They did not want to hear about the dumb childish news of my days. They wanted to talk about really important stuff that happened in high school or maybe in college or at work. So the only way I could get into a conversation was to say something funny. I think I must have done it accidentally at first, just accidentally made a pun that stopped the conversation, something of that sort. And then I found out that a joke was a way to break into an adult conversation.

I grew up at a time when comedy in this country was superb—it was the Great Depression. There were large numbers of absolutely top comedians on radio. And without intending to, I really studied them. I would listen to comedy at least an hour a night all through my youth, and I got very interested in what jokes were and how they worked.

When I'm being funny, I try not to offend. I don't think much of what I've done has been in really ghastly taste. I don't think I have embarrassed many people, or distressed them. The only shocks I use are an occasional obscene word. Some things aren't funny. I can't imagine a humorous book or skit about Auschwitz, for instance. And it's not possible for me to make a joke about the death of John F. Kennedy or Martin Luther King. Otherwise I can't think of any subject that I would steer away from, that I could do nothing with. Total catastrophes are terribly amusing, as Voltaire demonstrated. You know, the Lisbon earthquake is funny.

I saw the destruction of Dresden. I saw the city before and then came out of an air-raid shelter and saw it afterward, and certainly one response was laughter. God knows, that's the soul seeking some relief.

Scene2

In case you haven't noticed, we are now as feared and hated all over the world as the Nazis once were.

And with good reason.

In case you haven't noticed, our unelected leaders

A Man Without a Country

have dehumanized millions and millions of human beings simply because of their religion and race. We wound'em and kill'em and torture'em and imprison'em all we want.

Piece of cake.

In case you haven't noticed, we also dehumanized our own soldiers, not because of their religion or race, but because of their low social class.

Send'em anywhere. Make'em do anything.

Piece of cake.

The O'Reilly Factor.

So I am a man without a country, except for the librarians and a Chicago paper called *In These Times*.

Before we attacked Iraq, the majestic *New York Times* guaranteed that there were weapons of mass destruction there.

Albert Einstein and Mark Twain gave up on the

human race at the end of their lives, even though Twain hadn't even seen the First World War. War is now a form of TV entertainment, and what made the First World War so particularly entertaining were two American inventions, barbed wire and the machine gun.

Shrapnel was invented by an Englishman of the same name. Don't you wish you could have something named after you?

Like my distinct betters Einstein and Twain, I now give up on people, too. I am a veteran of the Second World War and I have to say this is not the first time I have surrendered to a pitiless war machine.

My last words? "Life is no way to treat an animal, not even a mouse."

Scene3

Humor is a way of holding off how awful life can be, to protect yourself. Finally, you get just too tired, and the news is too awful, and humor doesn't work anymore. Somebody like Mark Twain thought life was quite awful but held the awfulness at bay with jokes and so forth, but finally he couldn't do it anymore. His wife, his best friend, and two of his daughters had died. If you live long enough, a lot of people close to you are going to die.

It may be that I am no longer able to joke—that it is no longer a satisfactory defense mechanism. Some people are funny, and some are not. I used to be funny, and perhaps I'm not anymore. There may have been so many shocks and disappointments that the defense of humor no longer works. It may be that I have become rather grumpy because I've seen so many things that have offended me that I cannot deal with in terms of laughter.

This may have happened already. I really don't know what I'm going to become from now on. I'm simply along for the ride to see what happens to this body and this brain of mine. I'm startled that I became a writer. I don't think I can control my life or my writing. Every other writer I know feels he is steering himself, and I don't have that feeling. I don't have that sort of control. I'm simply becoming.

All I really wanted to do was give people the relief of laughing. Humor can be a relief, like an aspirin tablet. If a hundred years from now people are still laughing, I'd certainly be pleased.

9 オバマ演説集

難易度 ★★★

聴衆の心を動かす、
バラク・オバマ氏の卓越した「言葉の力」

> **原題** The Speeches of Barack Obama
> **発表** 2008年11月
> **内容**:『オバマ演説集』(小社刊)は、CNNで放送されたバラク・オバマの2004年7月の民主党大会基調演説、ヒラリー・クリントンと大統領候補指名争いを繰り広げた予備選中の2008年3月の演説、民主党大会で正式に大統領候補者として指名を受けた同年8月の指名受諾演説、本選で大統領に当選したときに行われた同年11月の勝利演説を収録。

オバマって誰だ?

　2009年1月、第四十四代アメリカ合衆国大統領に就任したバラク・オバマ氏は、アメリカで黒人初の大統領となりました。かつて差別の対象となったアフリカ系アメリカ人の中から、世界一の大国を指導する大統領が現れるとは、数十年前には誰も予想できなかったことでしょう。不可能だと思われたことが実現するところに、アメリカという国の果てしない可能性を感じます。

　2004年の大統領選の時点で、オバマ氏は民主党の上院議員選の

候補者にはなっていましたが、イリノイ州議会の新人議員に過ぎず、中央政界ではほとんど無名の存在でした。そのオバマ氏が一躍注目を浴びるきっかけとなったのが、同年7月に行われた党大会での基調演説です。

　オバマ氏が話し始めると「オバマって誰だ？」という会場の雰囲気が、期待と希望に満ちたものに変わっていきました。オバマ氏の言葉の力が、聴衆の心を動かしたのです。

完璧な構成のスピーチ

　彼はまず、自分の生い立ちから話を始めます。 **Scene1**

　祖父は、ケニアを植民地としていたイギリス人の使用人で、父親はケニアの村でヤギの世話をしながら成長しました。祖父は息子に大きな夢を託し、やがて父親は奨学金でハワイ大学に留学します。母親は、カンザス州のあまり裕福ではない家庭に生まれ、両親とともにハワイへ移り住みました。

　二人はハワイ大学で出会って結婚し、やがてオバマ氏が誕生します。彼らは、アメリカという国が与えてくれる可能性を信じて、自分たちの息子がアメリカで最高の学校に行くことを夢見ました。オバマ氏の演説は、アメリカという国が、生まれや学歴などと関係なくチャンスを与えてくれる国だということを、自分の生い立

ちを通して説きながら、アメリカ建国の理想に結びつけるという、きわめて完璧な構成をとっています。 Scene2

　この基調演説の内容は大変素晴らしいものでした。そして、それ以上に素晴らしかったのは、その演説を聞いてオバマ氏を重要な政治家として認めたアメリカの社会だと思います。2004年の時点でオバマ氏がほとんど無名であったにも関わらず、演説の内容が良かったからフェアに評価する。そういう精神がまだきちんと機能している国なのだと実感させられます。

人の心を動かす、オバマ氏の「言葉の力」

　わが国の場合は、そのような精神がほとんど育っていないところに、社会の行き詰まりの原因があるのかもしれません。また、政治家の演説という点から見ても、アメリカには遥かに及びません。終戦後、占領下の日本でGHQ最高司令官だったマッカーサーが「日本人の精神年齢は十二歳程度」と発言しましたが、今の日本人も「民主主義の成熟度」という観点から見ると、そう言わざるを得ないのではないかと思います。

　というのは、政治家の演説には内容が空虚なものが多く、たとえば「郵政民営化」や「友愛精神」といった政策やスローガンが、どのような政治的理想や原理原則に則っているのかという説明が

ありません。それを聞く国民やマスメディアも、評論家が言ったことをそのまま鵜呑みにするか、それに対して批判するだけです。

　オバマ氏の演説では、原理原則に裏打ちされた政治的理想がきちんと語られています。例えば **Scene3** では、何かと共和党と民主党に分けたがる評論家を批判しながら、民主主義の原理を説明していきます。

　「リベラルなアメリカも保守的なアメリカもありはしない——あるのはアメリカ合衆国」なのだと。当時のアメリカは、ブッシュ大統領によるイラク戦争の是非をめぐって賛成派と反対派に国が二分され、分裂状態に瀕していました。

　オバマ氏が演説を進めるにしたがい「この男は何者だ？」「素晴らしい」と聴衆の反応は変わっていき、最後には熱狂的な満場総立ちの拍手で埋め尽くされます。未来のアメリカ合衆国大統領が、華やかにデビューした瞬間でした。

アメリカという国が生んだ大統領

　2008年1月、民主党内での大統領候補指名争いとなる予備選がスタート。初の女性大統領を目指すヒラリー・クリントン氏と初のアフリカ系アメリカ人大統領を目指すオバマ氏との間で激しい指名争いが繰り広げられました。

ヒラリー氏が優勢な状況の中で行われた演説でも、オバマ氏は疲労や落胆を見せることなく、「yes, we can」のメッセージを発し続けます。 Scene4

　2008年8月、予備選に勝利したオバマ氏は民主党の大統領候補として正式に指名を受け、同年11月の本選では共和党のジョン・マケイン氏を大差で破ります。地元シカゴのグランドパークに集まった二十万人以上の聴衆の熱気と興奮に包まれる中、オバマ氏は勝利演説を行いました。 Scene5

　オバマ氏を当選させたのは、人種でも、お金でも、若さでもなく、その言葉に表れた政治思想の卓越です。オバマ氏は、どのようなヴィジョンを持ち、どのように語るかで政治のリーダーが決まる、アメリカという国が生んだ大統領なのだということです。

　マッカーサーが「日本人の精神年齢は十二歳程度」と発言した話を述べましたが、この発言は実は、成熟した民主主義を持ちながら、ファシズムに走ってしまったドイツと日本とを比べて、日本を擁護する文脈で述べられたものです。民主主義の成熟度において日本は十二歳の少年であり、理想を実現する余地はまだある、という意味で言ったのです。

　そう考えると、日本の未来は決して暗いものではないのではないでしょうか。

The Speeches of Barack Obama

オバマ演説集

Scene1

On behalf of the great state of Illinois, crossroads of a nation, Land of Lincoln, let me express my deepest gratitude for the privilege of addressing this convention. Tonight is a particular honor for me because, let's face it, my presence on this stage is pretty unlikely.

My father was a foreign student, born and raised in a small village in Kenya. He grew up herding goats, went to school in a tin-roof shack. His father—my grandfather—was a cook, a domestic servant to the British. But my grandfather had larger dreams for his son. Through hard work and perseverance my father got a scholarship to study in a magical place, America, that shone as a beacon of freedom and opportunity to so many who had come before.

While studying here, my father met my mother. She was born in a town on the other side of the world, in Kansas. Her father worked on oil rigs and farms through most of the Depression. The day after Pearl Harbor my grandfather signed up for duty, joined Patton's army, marched across Europe. Back home, my grandmother raised a baby and went to work on a bomber assembly line. After the war, they studied on the GI Bill, bought a house through FHA, and later moved west all the way to Hawaii in search of opportunity. And they, too, had big dreams for their daughter.

A common dream, born of two continents, my parents shared not only an improbable love, they shared an abiding faith in the possibilities of this nation. They would give me an African name, Barack, or "blessed," believing that in a tolerant America your name is no barrier to success. They imagined…they imagined me going to the best schools in the land, even though they weren't rich, because in a generous America you don't have to be rich to achieve your potential.

They're both passed away now. And yet, I know that on this night they do…look down on me with great pride. They stand here…And I stand here today, grateful for the diversity of my heritage, aware that my parents' dreams live on in my two precious daughters. I stand here knowing that my story is part of the larger American story, that I owe a debt to all of those who came before me, and that, in no other country on earth, is my story even possible.

Scene 2

Tonight, we gather to affirm the greatness of our Nation, not because of the height of our skyscrapers, or the power of our military, or the size of our economy. Our pride is based on a very simple premise, summed up in a declaration made over two hundred years ago: "We hold these truths to be self-evident, that all men are created equal, that they are endowed by their Creator with certain inalienable rights, that among these are life, liberty and the pursuit of happiness."

That is the true genius of America, a faith…a faith in simple dreams, an insistence on small miracles; that we can tuck in our children at night and know that they are fed and clothed and safe from harm; that we can say what we think, write what we think, without hearing a sudden knock on the door; that we can have an idea and start our own business without paying a bribe; that we can participate in the political process without fear of retribution, and that our votes will be counted—at least most of the time.

This year, in this election we are called to reaffirm our values and our commitments, to hold them against a hard reality and see how we're measuring up to the legacy of our forbearers and the promise of future generations.

Scene3

Now, even as we speak, there are those who are preparing to divide us—the spin masters, the negative ad peddlers who embrace the politics of "anything goes." Well, I say to them tonight, there is not a liberal America and a conservative America— there is the United States of America. There is not a Black America and a White America and Latino America and Asian America—there's the United States of America.

The pundits...the pundits like to slice-and-dice our country into Red States and Blue States; Red States for Republicans, Blue States for Democrats. But I've got news for them, too. We worship an "awesome God" in the Blue States, and we don't like federal agents poking around in our libraries in the Red States. We coach Little League in the Blue States, and, yes, we've got some gay friends in the Red States. There are patriots who opposed the war in Iraq, and there are patriots who supported the war in Iraq. We are one people, all of us pledging allegiance to the Stars and Stripes, all of us defending the United States of America.

Scene 4

John McCain and Hillary Clinton have echoed each other, dismissing this call for change as eloquent but empty, speeches not solutions. And yet they know, or they should know, that it's a call that did not begin with my words. It began with words that were spoken on the floors of factories in Ohio and across the deep plains of Texas, words that came from classrooms in South Carolina and living rooms in the state of Iowa, from first-time voters and lifelong cynics, from Democrats and Independents and Republicans alike.

The world is watching what we do here. The world is paying attention to how we conduct ourselves, what we say, how we treat one another. What will they see? What will we tell them? What will we show them? Can we come together across party and region, race and religion to restore prosperity and opportunity as the birthright of every American? Can we lead the community of nations in taking on the common threats of the 21st century—terrorism and climate change, genocide and disease? Can we send a message to all those weary travelers beyond our shores who long to be free from fear and want that the United States of America is and always will be the last best hope on earth? We say, we hope, we believe, yes, we can!

Scene5

Hello, Chicago.

If there is anyone out there who still doubts that America is a place where all things are possible, who still wonders if the dream of our founders is alive in our time, who still questions the power of our democracy, tonight is your answer.

It's the answer spoken by young and old, rich and poor, Democrat and Republican, black, white, Hispanic, Asian, Native American, gay, straight, disabled and not disabled—Americans who sent a message to the world that we have never been just a collection of individuals or a collection of Red States and Blue States. We are, and always will be, the United States of America.

It's the answer that led those who've been told for so long by so many to be cynical and fearful and doubtful about what we can achieve to put their hands on the arc of history and bend it once more toward the hope of a better day. It's been a long time coming, but tonight, because of what we did on this day in this election at this defining moment, change has come to America.

10 選択の自由

難易度 ★★☆

**強烈なイデオロギーを、
平易な英語で解き明かした書**

> 原題 Free to Choose
> 著者 Milton Friedman, Rose Friedman
> 発表 1980年
>
> 内容：アメリカの新自由主義のマクロ経済学者、ミルトン・フリードマンとその妻ローズによる、「急進的自由主義」を説いた書。市場の威力についてや、大恐慌の原因やインフレ論といったマクロ経済、社会保障や学校教育などについてのミクロの経済政策に関する提案を含む、フリードマンの思想の集大成とも言うべき内容。1976年のノーベル経済学賞受賞のきっかけとなった。

強烈な読書体験

　アメリカの経済学者ミルトン・フリードマン（Milton Friedman）の著作には専門的な内容のものが多いのですが、この『選択の自由』（Free to Choose）は一般の人々を対象にしたものだけあって、とてもわかりやすく書かれています。

　僕がこの本に出会ったのは、大学に入りたての十八歳の頃。出

版された直後に手に取ったことになります。その印象はとにかく強烈でした。それまで読んだ本では感じたことのない衝撃を受け、その後の僕の人生にも、非常に大きな影響を与えた本です。

ミルトン・フリードマンは「政府による有効需要（貨幣支出に裏づけられた需要）の管理が重要」だとするケインズ経済学に異を唱え、新しい経済理論を打ち立てた人物です。彼は世界大恐慌を体験しており、その経験から市場はできるかぎり政府が介入すべきではなく、自由な競争に任されるべきだという「マネタリズム」を提唱しています。

彼の主張が正しいかどうかの判断は別として、その急進的自由主義は1980年代にレーガン米大統領やサッチャー英首相によって現実の政策になり、日本の中曽根政権をはじめ世界各国の指導者の経済政策にも多大な影響を与えました。

具体的な事例で、わかりやすく説明

とにかく非常に強烈なイデオロギーを提示した本なのですが、そこで「すごい」と思わせるのが、それを一つ一つ徹底的に具体的な事例でわかりやすく説明している点です。「自由」や「競争」といった問題を論じるときにありがちな抽象論で終わることなく、強固な説得力で読者を圧倒します。

これほど強烈に一つの世界観を提示している人が、世の中にはいる——。そろそろ十代も終わりに差しかかろうとしていた僕にとって、そのスケールの大きさ、世界観の広さは圧倒的な迫力を持って迫ってきました。ちょうど、ニーチェの作品を読んだときの衝撃と似ているかもしれません。

　しかし、これも英語という言語の持つ明快さがあって、初めて成り立つ世界なのではないかと思います。つまり、読んでみればわかりますが、とてもわかりやすい言葉で書かれているのです。内容は広い世界を扱っていても、言葉自体は非常に平易で明快。複雑な構文や、もって回ったような表現で読者を苦しませることはありません。第一章「市場の威力」（The Power of the Market）の冒頭部分である **Scene1** を読んでもそれはわかります。

大人になった今、読み直したい一冊

　テーマは福祉や教育、労働者の権利について、インフレなどの経済問題についてなど、多岐にわたりますが、ここでは「平等」について書かれた箇所をご紹介しましょう。

　Scene2 は「結果の平等」という、二十世紀に入ってから西欧諸国の政策に影響を与えてきた概念について論じている非常に興味深い箇所です。これは「すべての人がゴールで同一線上に並

んでいなくてはならない」とする考え方で、「ほとんど宗教的信仰の対象とさえなってきている」というものです。ちなみに、52ページの "the other two"（他の二つの平等の概念）とは「神の前における平等」と「機会の平等」を指しています。

本書でも取り上げているルイス・キャロルの『不思議の国のアリス』で、びしょぬれになったアリスと動物たちが、体を乾かすためにレースを行う場面があります。レースはそれぞれが好きなときに走り出し、勝手にやめるという奇妙なものです。すっかり体が乾いてドードー鳥が競争の終わりを宣言すると、みんなが集まってきて「誰が勝ったんだ？」とたずねます。返事に窮したドードー鳥の答え――「全員が優勝。だから全員が賞品をもらわなくちゃ」というのが、「結果の平等」の考え方として引用されています。

このように "No nonsense"（ナンセンスの混じり得ない）なところが英語圏の文化の素晴らしいところだと思います。イデオロギーを語るときでも、読者を納得させられなければ意味はありません。ただ単に「自由」について長々と書き連ねているのではなく、言っていることが「地に足がついている」のです。大人になった今、もう一度しっかりと読み直してみたい一冊です。

Free to Choose

選択の自由

Scene 1

Every day each of us uses innumerable goods and services—to eat, to wear, to shelter us from the elements, or simply to enjoy. We take it for granted that they will be available when we want to buy them. We never stop to think how many people have played a part in one way or another in providing those goods and services. We never ask ourselves how it is that the corner grocery store—or nowadays, supermarket—has the items on its shelves that we want to buy, how it is that most of us are able to earn the money to buy those goods.

It is natural to assume that someone must give orders to make sure that the "right" products are produced in the "right" amounts and available at the "right" places. That is one method of coordinating the activities of a large number of people—the method of the army. The general gives orders to the colonel, the colonel to the major, the major to the lieutenant, the lieutenant to the sergeant, and the sergeant to the private.

Scene2

That different concept, equality of outcome, has been gaining ground in this century. It first affected government policy in Great Britain and on the European continent. Over the past half-century it has increasingly affected government policy in the United States as well. In some intellectual circles the desirability of equality of outcome has become an article of religious faith: everyone should finish the race at the same time. As the Dodo said in *Alice in Wonderland*, "*Everybody* has won, and *all* must have prizes."

For this concept, as for the other two, "equal" is not to be interpreted literally as "identical." No one really maintains that everyone, regardless of age or sex or other physical qualities, should have identical rations of each separate item of food, clothing, and so on. The goal is rather "fairness," a much vaguer notion—indeed, one that it is difficult, if not impossible, to define precisely. "Fair shares for all" is the modern slogan that has replaced Karl Marx's, "To each according to his needs, from each according to his ability."

This concept of equality differs radically from the other two. Government measures that promote personal equality or equality of opportunity enhance liberty; government measures to achieve "fair shares for all" reduce liberty. If what people get is to be determined by "fairness," who is to decide what is "fair"? As a chorus of voices asked the Dodo, "But who is to give the prizes?" "Fairness" is not an objectively determined concept once it departs from identity. "Fairness," like "needs," is in the eye of the beholder. If all are to have "fair shares," someone or some group of people must decide what shares are fair—and they must be able to impose their decisions on others, taking from those who have more than their "fair" share and giving to those who have less. Are those who make and impose such decisions equal to those for whom they decide? Are we not in George Orwell's *Animal Farm*, where "all animals are equal, but some animals are more equal than others"?

Column

「ネイティブ」信仰の呪縛から逃れ、"自由に"英語で表現する

ネイティブ礼賛主義から脱却する

　僕たちは何のために英語を勉強するのでしょうか。

　ネイティブのように話せるようになるためでしょうか、英文をスラスラと読めるようになるためでしょうか。ここで一つ大切なことは、「ネイティブのように話せること自体に価値はない」ということです。ただ「ネイティブのように」話すだけなら、どんなイギリス人だってアメリカ人だってできます。どの言語であれ、大切なのはその言語を使って「何を話すか」という問題です。

　日本人が英語を習得する意味、英語を使って何を世界に発信していくべきか――。この命題にヒントを与えてくれたのが、心理学者の河合隼雄さんです。"Individual in the Japanese cultural context"という短い論考の中で、河合さんは外国人に向けて、日本人の「個人」の概念について説明しています。

　西洋においては常にキリスト教的な「神の目線」が、人々の暮らしや

価値観に影響を及ぼし、それがいわゆる西洋的な「個人 (individual)」の概念を生み出してきました。しかし日本においては、こうした西洋的な「個人」の概念は発達してきませんでした。日本人にとっては当たり前の文化や風習も、海外から見ると一切がベールに包まれていたことを、河合さんは比較文化の観点から考察し、英語で丁寧に解き明かしています。

僕が英語でしていきたいこと

長い間締め切った部屋の窓を開け、新鮮な空気を入れて風通しを良くする——。このテキストを読んで僕が感じたのは、そのようなイメージです。日本という閉ざされた国の窓を開け、外に向かって日本人の考え方を紹介し、同時に外の風も引き入れる。これから僕が英語でしていきたいことは、まさにこういうことです。

英語と一言でいっても、僕が仕事で読んでいるような論文の英語もあれば、文学的な英語もある。あるいはブログやツイッターで使われているような、ブロークンな英語もあり、一方でインドやシンガポールで使われているような独特な英語もあります。

僕たちはそろそろ「ネイティブ」信仰の呪縛から解かれて、英語で"自由に"自分を表現していく、そんな「英語の下剋上」を起こすべきなのではないでしょうか。

11 三四郎 (Sanshirō)

難易度 ★☆☆

英語という言語で
漱石を読む意味について考える

原題　三四郎（Sanshirō）
著者　夏目漱石（Natsume Sōseki）
訳者　Jay Rubin
発表　1908年（英語版は2009年）

あらすじ：大学入学のために熊本から上京した三四郎にとって、見るもの、聞くものすべてが新しい驚きの連続であった。三四郎は聡明で自由気ままな女性、里見美禰子に出会い惹かれていくが、その想いをよそに美禰子は……。

僕にとっての夏目漱石

　僕が初めて読んだ漱石の作品は『吾輩は猫である』で小学校五年生のときでした。その後、『坊っちゃん』、『草枕』、『三四郎』、『こころ』などを読み進めていくうちに、漱石は自分にとってかけがえのない作家になっていきました。

　そして今回、「漱石を英語で読んでみたら、どのような味わいになるのだろうか」と思い、『三四郎』の英訳本を読みました。訳者

は、村上春樹さんの『ノルウェイの森』や『ねじまき鳥クロニクル』などの英訳で知られるジェイ・ルービンさん。ちなみに、Penguin Classicsから出ている『Sanshirō』では村上春樹さんが大変素晴らしい序論を書かれています。

英訳された『三四郎』を読むと、日本人がどうやって自分たちの世界を英語で表現して、「普遍化させていく」べきなのかという道筋が見えてきます。

青春のときめきと、自己批判

『三四郎』は、大学に入るために熊本から上京してきた青年、三四郎の青春のときめきと挫折の物語です。聡明にして自由気ままな里見美禰子への愛。「大論文を書く」と豪語しながら何もしない佐々木与次郎との友情。深い見識を持ちながら、世間的に恵まれない広田先生の教えなど。さまざまな人たちとの出会いを通して新しい世界に目が開かれていく三四郎の姿が描かれています。

この小説は、三四郎と美禰子の関係を中心に書かれたものですが、その中に日本文明を批判するという側面もきちんと描かれています。それが端的に現れているのが、上京する汽車の中で三四郎が広田先生と出会う場面です。 **Scene1**

三四郎がプラットホームにいた西洋人に見惚れていると、広田

先生が「どうも西洋人は美しいですね」と言います。三四郎が適当に受けていると、広田先生は続けて日本批判を始めます。

Scene2

この当時の日本は、日露戦争（明治37～38年）に勝って、国中が戦勝に沸いていました。そのような中で「日本は亡びる」と予言する広田先生の冷徹な目は、英国留学を経験し、西欧列強の底力を思い知らされた漱石の目に他なりません。

この自己批判の精神こそが漱石のすぐれた点で、自分の国や自分自身を客観的に見て、その長所や短所を見据えていかなければ真の発展は望めないのではないかと思います。

漱石を英訳で読むことの意味

『三四郎』を英語で読んでみて初めて気がついたことがありました。物語の中で美禰子は西洋風の絵画のモデルを務めるのですが、その絵を描いた画工の原口さんが「普通の日本の女ではモデルにはならない」といったことを広田先生に言うシーンがあります。日本語で読んでいるときは、それほど重要なシーンに思えなかったのですが、英語で読むと美禰子という女性が西洋的な美意識の中で絵の題材になり得るような、「新しい日本の女」として描かれていることがわかるのです。

漱石の作品は、言うまでもないことですが日本語の文体が優れています。ですが、逆に日本語の文体があまりにも素晴らしかったために、その方にばかり気をとられてこの小説が真に描いていたものに気がつきませんでした。それが英語に移し替えられたことによって、『三四郎』という小説の持っているドラマの骨格が見えてきたのです。

　英語という「普遍的な言語」を用いることによって、言葉を超えた物語の本質を考えることができたのだと思います。つまり、英語を学ぶことは、「言葉を越えた普遍性」を考える訓練にもなるのではないでしょうか。

Sanshirō

三四郎

Scene 1

As if by prearrangement, they both bought meals from the platform vendors in Hamamatsu. The train showed no sign of moving even after they had finished eating. Sanshirō noticed four or five Westerners strolling back and forth past the train window. One pair was probably a married couple; they were holding hands in spite of the hot weather. Dressed entirely in white, the woman was very beautiful. Sanshirō had never seen more than half a dozen foreigners in the course of his lifetime. Two of them were his teachers in college, and unfortunately one of those was a hunchback. He knew one woman, a missionary. She had a pointed face like a smelt or a barracuda. Foreigners as colorful and attractive as these were not only something quite new for Sanshirō, they seemed to be of a higher class. He stared at them, entranced. Arrogance from people like this was understandable. He went so far as to imagine himself traveling to the West and feeling insignificant among them. When the couple passed his window he tried hard to listen to their conversation, but he could make out none of it. Their pronunciation was nothing like that of his Kumamoto teachers.

Scene 2

"We Japanese are sad-looking things next to them. We can beat the Russians, we can become a 'first-class power,' but it doesn't make any difference. We still have the same faces, the same feeble little bodies. Just look at the houses we live in, the gardens we build around them. They're just what you'd expect from faces like this. —Oh yes, this is your first trip to Tokyo, isn't it? You've never seen Mount Fuji. We go by it a little farther on. Have a look. It's the finest thing Japan has to offer, the only thing we have to boast about. The trouble is, of course, it's just a natural object. It's been sitting there for all time. We didn't make it." He grinned broadly once again.

Sanshirō had never expected to meet anyone like this after Japan's victory in the Russo-Japanese War. The man was almost not Japanese, he felt.

"But still," Sanshirō argued, "Japan will start developing from now on at least."

"Japan is going to perish," the man replied coolly.

Anyone who dared say such a thing in Kumamoto would have been beaten on the spot, perhaps even arrested for treason. Sanshirō had grown up in an atmosphere that gave his mind no room at all for inserting an idea like this. Could the man be toying with him, taking advantage of his youth? The man was still grinning, but he spoke with complete detachment. Sanshirō did not know what to make of him. He decided to say nothing.

But then the man said, "Tokyo is bigger than Kumamoto. And Japan is bigger than Tokyo. And even bigger than Japan…" He paused and looked at Sanshirō, who was listening intently now. "Even bigger than Japan is the inside of your head. Don't even surrender yourself—not to Japan, not to anything. You may think that what you're doing is for the sake of the nation, but let something take possession of you like that, and all you do is bring it down."

12 賢者の贈りもの

絶妙なストーリーを紡ぐ短編の名手、オー・ヘンリーの代表作

原題　The Gift of the Magi
著者　O. Henry
発表　1905年

あらすじ：貧しい若夫婦が、相手にクリスマスプレゼントを買うお金を工面しようとする。妻は夫が大切にしている懐中時計を吊るす鎖を買うために髪を切り、売ってしまう。一方、夫は妻が欲しがっていたべっ甲のくしを買うために、自慢の懐中時計を売ってしまっていた。

絶妙なプロットと意外な結末

　オー・ヘンリー（O. Henry）は、アメリカを代表する短編小説家の一人です。彼の作品の特徴は、独特のユーモアと哀愁、それを効果的に伝える絶妙なプロット、そして巧妙に工夫された意外な結末にあります。それはまさに、「オー・ヘンリー流」と呼べるような独特の型をつくり上げています。

　オー・ヘンリーは、小説のテーマとして主に1900年代のニュー

ヨーク庶民の哀歓を描いて爆発的な人気を得ました。短編の名手としてアメリカのみならず世界にその名をとどろかせ、生涯で272編の短編作品を残しました。

『賢者の贈りもの』（The Gift of the Magi）は、新約聖書で東方の賢者がキリストの誕生を祝って贈りものを持ってきたエピソードが下敷きとなっているため、クリスマス劇の演目としても人気があり、作品としての知名度も非常に高いものになっています。

夫婦が用意したプレゼントとは

主人公は安アパートに住む貧乏な若夫婦、ジムとデラ。妻のデラは、明日はクリスマスだというのに、ジムに贈りものを買うお金がないことを嘆きます。そこで、彼女は自分の美しい髪を売ってお金を工面し、ジムが祖父と父から受け継いで大切にしている金の懐中時計を吊るすための鎖を買います。

その晩、仕事から帰ってきたジムは、短くなったデラの髪を見て呆然とその場に立ち尽くします。 **Scene1**

妻のデラは、自分の髪を売って夫の時計鎖を買いますが、一方の夫ジムは、妻がほしがっていたべっ甲のくしを買うために、自慢の懐中時計を売ってしまっていたのでした。 **Scene2**

オー・ヘンリーの文章表現に学ぶ

　オー・ヘンリーの文章は表現が非常にシンプルで、長さも一編が数ページ程度なので、さらっと読めます。ところが、オー・ヘンリーのような文章を英語で書けるかと言うと、これがなかなか難しいのです。

　よく言われることですが、日本人の書く英文はどうしても説明調でくどくなってしまいがちです。日本語という言語自体が、シンプルでストレートな表現をするようにはなっていないということも背景にあるのでしょう。英語の表現には簡素さが求められます。その意味からも、オー・ヘンリーの文章表現に学ぶところは大きいと言えます。

The Gift of the Magi

賢者の贈りもの

Scene 1

Jim stopped inside the door, as immovable as a setter at the scent of quail. His eyes were fixed upon Della, and there was an expression in them that she could not read, and it terrified her. It was not anger, nor surprise, nor disapproval, nor horror, nor any of the sentiments that she had been prepared for. He simply stared at her fixedly with that peculiar expression on his face.

Della wriggled off the table and went for him. "Jim, darling," she cried, "don't look at me that way. I had my hair cut off and sold it because I couldn't have lived through Christmas without giving you a present. It'll grow out again—you won't mind, will you? I just had to do it. My hair grows awfully fast. Say 'Merry Christmas!' Jim, and let's be happy. You don't know what a nice—what a beautiful, nice gift I've got for you."

"You've cut off your hair?" asked Jim, laboriously, as if he had not arrived at that patent fact yet even after the hardest mental labor.

"Cut it off and sold it," said Della. "Don't you like me just as well, anyhow? I'm me without my hair, ain't I?"

Jim looked about the room curiously.

"You say your hair is gone?" he said with an air almost of idiocy.

"You needn't look for it," said Della. "It's sold, I tell you—sold and gone, too. It's Christmas Eve, boy. Be good to me, for it went for you. Maybe the hairs of my head were numbered," she went on with a sudden serious sweetness, "but nobody could ever count my love for you. Shall I put the chops on, Jim?"

Scene2

Jim drew a package from his overcoat pocket and threw it upon the table.

"Don't make any mistake, Dell," he said, "about me. I don't think there's anything in the way of a haircut or a shave or a shampoo that could make me like my girl any less. But if you'll unwrap that package you may see why you had me going a while at first."

White fingers and nimble tore at the string and paper. And then an ecstatic scream of joy; and then, alas! a quick feminine change to hysterical tears and wails, necessitating the immediate employment of all the comforting powers of the lord of the flat.

For there lay The Combs—the set of combs, side

and back, that Della had worshipped for long in a Broadway window. Beautiful combs, pure tortoise-shell, with jewelled rims—just the shade to wear in the beautiful vanished hair. They were expensive combs, she knew, and her heart had simply craved and yearned over them without the least hope of possession. And now, they were hers, but the tresses that should have adorned the coveted adornments were gone.

But she hugged them to her bosom, and at length she was able to look up with dim eyes and a smile and say: "My hair grows so fast, Jim!"

And then Della leaped up like a little singed cat and cried, "Oh, oh!"

Jim had not yet seen his beautiful present. She held it out to him eagerly upon her open palm. The dull precious metal seemed to flash with a reflection of her bright and ardent spirit.

"Isn't it a dandy, Jim? I hunted all over town to find it. You'll have to look at the time a hundred times a day now. Give me your watch. I want to see how it looks on it."

Instead of obeying, Jim tumbled down on the couch and put his hands under the back of his head and smiled.

"Dell," said he, "let's put our Christmas presents away and keep 'em a while. They're too nice to use just at present. I sold the watch to get the money to buy your combs. And now suppose you put the chops on."

13 魔女のパン

難易度 ★★☆

皮肉な結末をむかえる、中年女性のほろ苦いラブストーリー

原題	Witches' Loaves
著者	O. Henry
発表	1904〜1905年

あらすじ：パン屋を営むミス・マーサは、いつも古いパンしか買っていかない中年の男に惹かれ始める。男を貧乏な画家だと思い込んだミス・マーサは、ある日内緒でバターを塗ったパンを男に渡す。しかし結末は意外なことに……。

貧乏画家に寄せるひそかな恋心

ミス・マーサは、通りの角で小さなパン屋を営む中年女性です。階段を三段のぼって、ドアを開けるとベルがチリンと鳴る店と言えば、どんな店かだいたい想像がつくでしょう。

彼女は週に二、三回やってくる中年の男にひそかに恋心を抱き始めます。男は眼鏡をかけ、丁寧に刈りこまれた茶色のあご髭を持ち、強いドイツ訛りの英語を話しました。服はしわだらけでと

ころどころ擦り切れてはいましたが、いつも清潔で礼儀正しい人物です。そして、買っていくのは決まって売れ残りの古いパンでした。

あるとき、ミス・マーサは男の指に赤と茶色のしみがついていることに気がつき、彼はとても貧乏な画家なのだと思います。

Scene1 **Scene2**

ミス・マーサは男のことを気の毒に思い、ある日パンに切りこみを入れ、中にバターをたっぷり塗りこんで渡しました。

「大胆すぎたかしら？　あの人を怒らせやしなかったかしら」

ミス・マーサは頰を染めて男がこのことを発見するところを想像しながら、一日中そのことばかり考えていました。ところが……。

Scene3

ミス・マーサの心遣いは、裏目に出てしまいます。画家だと思っていた男は実は製図家で、古いパンは設計図の鉛筆の線を消すために使われていたものだったのです。男は「バターのせいで設計図が台無しになった」とミス・マーサに罵声を浴びせて帰っていくという、ほろ苦くも皮肉な話です。

余韻が残る、さらっとした文体

この物語の最後は、次のような文章で終わっています。

「ミス・マーサは店の奥に入って行った。そして水玉模様の絹のブラウスを脱いで、いつも着ていた古い茶色の服にかえた。それから、マルメロの実とホウ砂の混合物を窓からごみ入れの中に捨てた。」

Scene4

オー・ヘンリーは主人公の主観を描くとき、そこに深い想いや感情があったとしても、それを主人公の行動を通した客観的な文体でさらっと描きます。

僕はこれほど簡潔な表現で書かれている日本語の小説を見たことがない気がします。この作品も、日本語訳からは物足りない印象を受けてしまうのですが、英語で読むと物足りないどころか、むしろ余韻が残る文章になっています。そういう意味では「英語における余韻とは何なのか」を考えさせられる作品です。

Witches' Loaves

魔女のパン

Scene 1 CD2 18

Two or three times a week a customer came in in whom she began to take an interest. He was a middle-aged man, wearing spectacles and a brown beard trimmed to a careful point.

He spoke English with a strong German accent. His clothes were worn and darned in places, and wrinkled and baggy in others. But he looked neat, and had very good manners.

He always bought two loaves of stale bread. Fresh bread was five cents a loaf. Stale ones were two for five. Never did he call for anything but stale bread.

Once Miss Martha saw a red and brown stain on his fingers. She was sure then that he was an artist and very poor. No doubt he lived in a garret, where he painted pictures and ate stale bread and thought of the good things to eat in Miss Martha's bakery.

Often when Miss Martha sat down to her chops and light rolls and jam and tea she would sigh, and wish that the gentle-mannered artist might share her tasty meal instead of eating his dry crust in that draughty attic.

Scene 2

Often now when he came he would chat for a while across the showcase. He seemed to crave Miss Martha's cheerful words.

He kept on buying stale bread. Never a cake, never a pie, never one of her delicious Sally Lunns.

She thought he began to look thinner and discouraged. Her heart ached to add something good to eat to his meagre purchase, but her courage failed at the act. She did not dare affront him. She knew the pride of artists.

Miss Martha took to wearing her blue-dotted silk waist behind the counter. In the back room she cooked a mysterious compound of quince seeds and borax. Ever so many people use it for the complexion.

Scene 3

The front door bell jangled viciously. Somebody was coming in, making a great deal of noise.

Miss Martha hurried to the front. Two men were there. One was a young man smoking a pipe—a man she had never seen before. The other was her artist.

His face was very red, his hat was on the back of his head, his hair was wildly rumpled. He clinched his two fists and shook them ferociously at Miss Martha. *At Miss Martha.*

"*Dummkopf!*" he shouted with extreme loudness; and then "*Tausendonfer!*" or something like it, in German.

The young man tried to draw him away.

"I vill not go," he said angrily, "else I shall told her."

He made a bass drum of Miss Martha's counter.

"You haf shpoilt me," he cried, his blue eyes blazing behind his spectacles. "I vill tell you. You vas von *meddingsome old cat!*"

Miss Martha leaned weakly against the shelves and laid one hand on her blue-dotted silk waist. The young man took his companion by the collar.

"Come on," he said, "you've said enough." He dragged the angry one out at the door to the sidewalk, and then came back.

"Guess you ought to be told, ma'am," he said, "what the row is about. That's Blumberger. He's an architectural draughtsman. I work in the same office with him.

"He's been working hard for three months drawing a plan for a new city hall. It was a prize competition. He finished inking the lines yesterday. You know, a draughtsman always makes his drawing in pencil first. When it's done he rubs out the pencil lines with handfuls of stale breadcrumbs. That's better than india-rubber...."

Scene4

Miss Martha went into the back room. She took off the blue-dotted silk waist and put on the old brown serge she used to wear. Then she poured the quince seed and borax mixture out of the window into the ash can.

14 最後の一葉

難易度 ★★★

**最後の一枚の葉がモチーフの、
あまりに有名な短編小説の傑作**

原題	The Last Leaf
著者	O. Henry
発表	1905年

あらすじ：友人のスーとアパートに住むジョンジーは、肺炎になり生きる気力を失う。ジョンジーは窓から見える壁の蔦の葉を数え、最後の葉が散ってしまうとき自分も死ぬのだと言う。激しい風雨が吹き荒れた翌朝、壁には一枚の葉がへばりつくようにして残っていた。

芸術家の娘たちと老画家

ワシントン・スクエアの西側にある、グリニッチ・ヴィレッジ地区には芸術家たちが集う「芸術家村」があり、その一角にある煉瓦造りの古めかしいアパートに、スーとジョンジーという若い芸術家の娘が共同のアトリエを持って暮らしていました。二人は食堂で定食を食べているときに出会い、意気投合した仲です。

11月になったある日、ジョンジーは肺炎を患ってしまいます。

スーは医者から、「ジョンジーは生きる気力を失っている。このままでは助かる見込みは十に一つ」と告げられます。

心身ともに弱ったジョンジーは窓の外に見える、煉瓦の壁を這う蔦の葉を数え、「最後の一枚が落ちるとき、私も一緒にさよならするわ」と投げやりな言葉を吐くのでした。 Scene1

一方、彼女たちの階下に住む老画家のベールマンは、口癖のように「いつか傑作を描いてみせる」と豪語するものの着手さえせず、酒びたりの日々を送っていました。スーはベールマンに、ジョンジーが「蔦の葉が落ちたら死ぬ」と思い込んでいることを話します。ベールマンは酒の匂いをぷんぷんさせながら、ジョンジーの思い込みを「馬鹿げてる！」と罵ります。

その晩、激しい風雨が吹き荒れ、朝になると蔦の葉は最後の一枚になっていました。次の夜も北風が吹きつけ、激しい雨を降らせましたが、翌朝になっても最後の一枚の葉はまだ壁に残っています。 Scene2

落ちることのなかった、最後の葉

最後に残った葉は、ベールマンが嵐の中、煉瓦の壁に絵筆で描いたものだったのです。その葉のおかげでジョンジーは生きる気力を取りもどしますが、ベールマンは肺炎になり、「最後の一葉」

The Last Leaf | 81

を描いた二日後に亡くなります。真実を知ったスーは、この最後の一葉こそがベールマンがいつか描いてみせると言い続けた傑作なのだ、と評します。 Scene3

　モチーフとなっている最後の一枚の葉が落ちることと人の命を結びつける発想は、どこの国にでもあるものです。それを万人に通用するドラマの型に作り上げた先駆けが、オー・ヘンリーと言えるのではないでしょうか。そして、その独特のアメリカ的な型のバリエーションが無限にあることで、オー・ヘンリーは世界中で読まれ続けています。

The Last Leaf

最後の一葉

Scene 1 CD2 22

Johnsy's eyes were open wide. She was looking out the window and counting—counting backward.

"Twelve," she said, and a little later "eleven"; and then "ten," and "nine"; and then "eight" and "seven," almost together.

Sue looked solicitously out of the window. What was there to count? There was only a bare, dreary yard to be seen, and the blank side of the brick house twenty feet away. An old, old ivy vine, gnarled and decayed at the roots, climbed half way up the brick wall. The cold breath of autumn had stricken its leaves from the vine until its skeleton branches clung, almost bare, to the crumbling bricks.

"What is it, dear?" asked Sue.

"Six," said Johnsy, in almost a whisper. "They're falling faster now. Three days ago there were almost a hundred. It made my head ache to count them. But now it's easy. There goes another one. There are only five left now."

"Five what, dear? Tell your Sudie."

"Leaves. On the ivy vine. When the last one falls I must go, too. I've known that for three days. Didn't the doctor tell you?"

"Oh, I never heard of such nonsense," complained Sue, with magnificent scorn. "What have old ivy leaves to do with your getting well? And you used to love that vine, so, you naughty girl. Don't be a goosey. Why, the doctor told me this morning that your chances for getting well real soon were—let's see exactly what he said—he said the chances were ten to one! Why, that's almost as good a chance as we have in New York when we ride on the street cars or walk past a new building. Try to take some broth now, and let Sudie go back to her drawing, so she can sell the editor man with it, and buy port wine for her sick child, and pork chops for her greedy self."

Scene2　CD2 23

When Sue awoke from an hour's sleep the next morning she found Johnsy with dull, wide-open eyes staring at the drawn green shade.

"Pull it up; I want to see," she ordered, in a whisper.

Wearily Sue obeyed.

But, lo! after the beating rain and fierce gusts of wind that had endured through the livelong night, there yet stood out against the brick wall one ivy leaf. It was the last one on the vine. Still dark green near its stem, but with its serrated edges tinted with the yellow of dissolution and decay, it hung bravely from a branch some twenty feet above the ground.

"It is the last one," said Johnsy. "I thought it would surely fall during the night. I heard the wind. It will fall to-day, and I shall die at the same time."

"Dear, dear!" said Sue, leaning her worn face down to the pillow, "think of me, if you won't think of yourself. What would I do?"

But Johnsy did not answer. The lonesomest thing in all the world is a soul when it is making ready to go on its mysterious, far journey. The fancy seemed to possess her more strongly as one by one the ties that bound her to friendship and to earth were loosed.

Scene 3

Johnsy lay for a long time looking at it. And then she called to Sue, who was stirring her chicken broth over the gas stove.

"I've been a bad girl, Sudie," said Johnsy. "Something has made that last leaf stay there to show me how wicked I was. It is a sin to want to die. You may bring me a little broth now, and some milk with a little port in it, and—no; bring me a hand-mirror first, and then pack some pillows about me, and I will sit up and watch you cook."

An hour later she said:

"Sudie, some day I hope to paint the Bay of Naples."

The doctor came in the afternoon, and Sue had an excuse to go into the hallway as he left.

"Even chances," said the doctor, taking Sue's thin, shaking hand in his. "With good nursing you'll win. And now I must see another case I have downstairs. Behrman, his name is—some kind of an artist, I believe. Pneumonia, too. He is an old, weak man, and the attack is acute. There is no hope for him; but he goes to the hospital to-day to be made more comfortable."

The next day the doctor said to Sue: "She's out of danger. You've won. Nutrition and care now—that's all."

And that afternoon Sue came to the bed where Johnsy lay, contentedly knitting a very blue and very useless woolen shoulder scarf, and put one arm around her, pillows and all.

"I have something to tell you, white mouse," she said. "Mr. Behrman died of pneumonia to-day in the hospital. He was ill only two days. The janitor found him on the morning of the first day in his room downstairs helpless with pain. His shoes and clothing were wet through and icy cold. They couldn't imagine where he had been on such a dreadful night. And then they found a lantern, still lighted, and a ladder that had been dragged from its place, and some scattered brushes, and a palette with green and yellow colors mixed on it, and—look out the window, dear, at the last ivy leaf on the wall. Didn't you wonder why it never fluttered or moved when the wind blew? Ah, darling, it's Behrman's masterpiece—he painted it there the night that the last leaf fell."

FREE TO CHOOSE
Excerpt from FREE TO CHOOSE: A PERSONAL STATEMENT, copyright©1980 by Milton Friedman and Rose D. Friedman,
reprinted by permisison of Houghton Mifflin Harcourt Publishing Company through Tuttle-Mori Agency, Inc. Tokyo.
This material may not be reproduced in any form or by any means without the prior written permission of the publisher.

SANSHIRŌ
by Soseki Natsume, with an introduction by Haruki Murakami and translated with notes by Jay Rubin (Penguin Classics 2009).
Translation, Chronology, Further Reading and Notes copyright©Jay Rubin, 2009.
Introduction copyright©Haruki Murakami, 2009.
Reproduced by permission of Penguin Books Ltd. through Tuttle-Mori Agency, Inc.

BACKGROUND TO BRITAIN
by M.D.Munro Mackenzie and L.J. Westwood
©M.D.Munro Mackenzie and L.J. Westwood 1965

A MAN WITHOUT A COUNTRY
by Kurt Vonnegut
Copyright©2005 by Kurt Vonnegut
Excerpted from A Man Without A Country. Originally published by Seven Stories Press, New York.

INDIVIDUALS IN THE JAPANESE CULTURAL CONTEXT
by Kawai Hayao
54ページのコラムで取り上げた河合隼雄氏の論考は
「Asia-Pacific Review, Vol.6, No.2, 1999」に掲載されたものです。

Profile

茂木健一郎（もぎけんいちろう）

脳科学者。ソニーコンピュータサイエンス研究所シニアリサーチャー、慶應義塾大学大学院システムデザイン・マネジメント研究科特別研究教授。1962年、東京生まれ。東京大学理学部、法学部卒業後、東京大学大学院理学系研究科物理学専攻課程修了。理学博士。理化学研究所、ケンブリッジ大学を経て現職。専門は脳科学、認知科学。「クオリア」（感覚の持つ質感）をキーワードとして脳と心の関係を研究するとともに、文芸評論、美術評論にも取り組んでいる。2005年、『脳と仮想』（新潮社）で、第4回小林秀雄賞を受賞。2009年、『今、ここからすべての場所へ』（筑摩書房）で第12回桑原武夫学芸賞を受賞。「CNN English Express」（毎月6日発売、小社刊）にて「茂木健一郎の壁を超える！英語勉強法」好評連載中。

Staff

デザイン	大下賢一郎
DTP	メディアアート
写真	牧野明神
ルビ訳校閲	Evelyn Corbett
編集協力	石井綾子、三浦愛美、河野美香子、野澤真一
CD朗読	Chris Koprowski、Helen Morrison
CD録音・編集	ELEC（財団法人英語教育協議会）
編集	仁藤輝夫、谷岡美佐子、高野夏奈

モギケンの英語シャワーBOX 実践版
STEP2

2010年11月15日　初版第1刷発行
2013年5月1日　初版第7刷発行

著者	茂木健一郎
発行者	原　雅久
発行所	株式会社 朝日出版社
	〒101-0065　東京都千代田区西神田3-3-5
	電話　03-3263-3321（代表）
	http://www.asahipress.com
印刷・製本	図書印刷株式会社

ISBN978-4-255-00554-6
乱丁・落丁本はお取り替えいたします。
無断で複写複製することは著作権の侵害になります。
定価は外箱に表示してあります。

©Kenichiro Mogi 2010
Printed in Japan